100 QUESTIONS about CATS

and all the answers too!

Written and Illustrated by
Simon Abbott

PETER PAUPER PRESS, INC.
White Plains, New York

For Sheila, Brian, Indy, and Caspian

PETER PAUPER PRESS

In 1928, at the age of twenty-two, Peter Beilenson began printing books on a small press in the basement of his parents' home in Larchmont, New York. Peter—and later, his wife, Edna—sought to create fine books that sold at "prices even a pauper could afford."

Today, still family owned and operated, Peter Pauper Press continues to honor our founders' legacy of quality, value, and fun for big kids and small kids alike.

Library of Congress Cataloging-in-Publication Data

Names: Abbott, Simon, 1967- author, illustrator.
Title: 100 questions about cats : and all the answers too! / written and illustrated by Simon Abbott.
Other titles: One hundred questions about cats
Description: White Plains, New York : Peter Pauper Press, [2021] | Series: 100 questions about... | Audience: Ages 7+ | Audience: Grades K-1 | Summary: "In this illustrated educational guide, readers are introduced to all things cats-from the history of their domestication to cat care tips-through a series of questions and answers. Also included are facts about common breeds and famous cats, as well as cat-themed jokes"-- Provided by publisher.
Identifiers: LCCN 2020034123 | ISBN 9781441335364 (hardcover)
Subjects: LCSH: Cats--Juvenile literature.
Classification: LCC SF445.7 .A23 2021 | DDC 636.8--dc23
LC record available at https://lccn.loc.gov/2020034123

Designed by Heather Zschock

Text and illustrations copyright © 2021 by Simon Abbott

Published by Peter Pauper Press, Inc.
202 Mamaroneck Avenue
White Plains, New York 10601 USA

Published in the United Kingdom and Europe by Peter Pauper Press, Inc.
c/o White Pebble International
Unit 2, Plot 11 Terminus Rd.
Chichester, West Sussex PO19 8TX, UK

ISBN 978-1-4413-3536-4
Manufactured for Peter Pauper Press, Inc.
Printed in China

7 6 5 4 3 2 1

Visit us at www.peterpauper.com

Curious about cats?
Fascinated by fluffy felines?
Then this is the book for you!

How do cats use their whiskers?

Why did the ancient Egyptians
worship a cat goddess?

Which fur-midable feline has
the longest tail?

Let's leap in and find the answers to these
questions, and discover many more facts
about our furry friends!

FROM HEAD TO TAIL

Let's explore a cat's fantastic features, and find out how these creatures operate.

How well do cats hear?
Each ear has around 30 muscles, allowing it to rotate and swivel independently. When a cat hears an interesting noise, it can point its ears in the sound's direction. Cats can also hear higher and lower frequencies (or higher- and lower-pitched sounds) than humans, which helps them detect a wide range of prey and avoid their own predators.

Why do cats' eyes glow in the dark?
Cats have a layer of reflective cells in their eyes, called the tapetum lucidum (*tap-ee-tum lu-si-dum*), which allows their eyes to capture more light than non-shiny human eyes. Their pupils also open wider in the dark, which lets in more light to bounce off the tapetum lucidum and allows hungry cats to hunt at night.

What do cats use their whiskers for?

These highly-sensitive hairs help cats find their way in the dark, work out whether they can fit into small spaces, and detect small prey right under their noses. At the root of each whisker is a follicle packed with nerves which gives the cat information about air currents, as well as the size, texture, and location of any object.

How good is a cat's nose?

It's about fourteen times better than yours! A cat has 200 million scent-sensitive cells in its nose, compared to a human's mere 5 million. That's not to be sniffed at!

Why is a cat's tongue a little scratchy?

Two reasons! First, the rough tongue acts like a comb to keep their fur well-groomed and scent-free, which makes it harder for predators to track them down and prey to smell when they're coming. Second, they use the scratchy spikes on their tongues to scrape meat from the bones of their meals. Very practical!

We've looked at the top end—now for the rest of the body! Does a cat's tail have an important function?

A cat uses its tail to balance and to show its mood. The flexible, whip-like tail is an extension of the cat's spine, made of around 20 bones called **vertebrae** surrounded by muscles, ligaments, and tendons. This allows the cat to lift its tail, move it side to side, or swish it down between its back legs.

Why does a cat always seem to land on its feet?

That's thanks to its "righting reflex." Take a look:

1. Fluid- and nerve-filled structures within the inner ear tell the cat which way is up.

2. The cat rotates its head to check out where it's going to land.

3. The cat's super-flexible spine lets it twist and turn over while falling.

4. The cat arranges its front feet under its body, with its paws protecting its face from impact.

How can cats squeeze themselves into tiny spaces?

They have tiny collarbones, which are joined to the shoulder blades with flexible muscle instead of rigid bone like yours are. This helps them fit through gaps no bigger than their heads!

What gives cats the strength to leap so far?

Cats make first-rate jumpers because of their long, muscle-packed back legs, which they "wind up" by crouching, then springing up like, well, a spring. An average cat can vault up to six times its height!

Why do cats have retractable claws?

Cats' claws are tools used to climb, defend themselves, and catch and hold prey. A cat can draw back its claws to keep them sharp and prevent them from catching on things.

CAT COMMUNICATIONS

How do our cats communicate with us? Let's decode kitty body language and sounds!

What is the best way to judge a cat's mood?
Take a look at its tail. If it's held high, then the cat is feeling confident and (if the tip is bent) friendly. If the tail is curled around your legs or another cat's tail, then the cat is being affectionate. An insecure or nervous cat will tuck its tail between its legs, and a cat that's about to attack will swish its tail back and forth. A tense, upright tail with the fur sticking up means the cat is feeling threatened. Time to back off!

Do cats really prefer it when you ignore them?
Cats find direct eye contact alarming, whether it's from a human or another animal. On the other hand, we humans tend to look directly at things that interest us and, well, ignore things that don't. So yes, to a cat, people who don't stare make the best company. Guess grown-ups were right when they said it's impolite to stare!

Why does a cat roll over and show its tummy?

Sometimes, a cat is showing great trust. It feels comfortable and safe enough around you to roll over and relax. But take care! In the wild, a cat will roll over in a defensive posture, allowing it to use all its teeth and claws to fight an attacker, and just because your kitty is exposing its belly doesn't mean it enjoys belly rubs. Take care when reaching over to pet your cat, or else you may end up with an arm full of claws!

How do cats communicate with their eyes?

If a cat blinks slowly, it's expressing trust and affection. It can use a long, unblinking stare to intimidate fellow felines and control its territory. A cat will squint to protect its eyes from the claws of a potential attacker, and large, round pupils indicate fear or signal that the cat is about to attack.

Why do cats meow?

Many different reasons! Kittens meow to catch their mothers' watchful eyes. It's their way to say they need something, be it food, warmth, protection, or just attention.

That's understandable! But why do adult cats vocalize?
As kittens grow older, they meow to other cats less and less often. However, they'll meow to humans like you and me to tell us they're hungry, sick, lonely, stressed, confused, or just happy to see us!

Do some cats meow more than others?

Siamese cats are pretty talkative, and on occasion can talk all day (and all night) long!

What does it mean when cats purr?

Although cats purr to communicate how content they are, some kitties also use purring to soothe themselves when they are stressed or uncomfortable. The purr causes vibrations within the cat's body, which helps breathing, heals injuries, builds muscle, and eases pain.

How loud can a cat purr?

The average cat purrs at a peaceful 25 decibels (a way of measuring the loudness of sound). However, let's meet Merlin, whose record-breaking purring has hit 67.8 decibels—almost as loud as a dishwasher! Pass the ear plugs!

CLEVER CATS

When it comes to animal aptitude, is the feline species fur-midable or a downright cat-astrophe? Let's get the low-down!

Just how smart are cats?

It's hard to confirm, as cats don't like being told what to do, even when they take part in scientific experiments. What we do know is that the structure of a cat's brain is 90% similar to the structure of the human brain . . . and we're pretty smart, right?

Are cats smarter than dogs?

That's also a hard question to answer, as cats refuse to take part in the same tests! Let's look at some evidence instead. A part of everyone's brain called the cerebral cortex is responsible for things like thinking, speech, and memory as well as sight, hearing, smell, and touch. In this part of the brain, cats have 300 million neurons (brain cells) compared to dogs' 160 million. So it's thought that cats have a better memory and superior problem-solving abilities compared to dogs.

So cats are clever! Why don't we have any sheep-herding cats, police cats, and seeing-eye cats?

Cats are aloof and impatient. If they think an activity isn't worth doing, they'll wander off and do something else. That includes important jobs, like guiding their owners through busy streets! Domestic dogs have been trained to respond to a treat or reward for thousands of years, so they'll happily perform almost any task in response to praise from their owners.

Do we have a winner in the Cunning Cat vs. Clever Canine Competition? Let's call it a draw! Dogs obviously have greater social intelligence (meaning they're more attuned to others and easier to train), and cats make exceptional problem-solvers.

Why are cats so hard to train?

They are self-interested, independent animals, so they're resistant to obedience classes! Still, cats can be trained to perform some tasks, as long as there is an immediate reward or the tricks you want them to do already fit their catty profile. For instance, cats can be trained to catch mice . . . if they don't already do that on their own!

Are there any exceptions to this rule?

Sure! Let's look at Nora, the piano-playing pussycat. After observing her music teacher owner and her students, this talented cat hopped up onto the bench and started playing the piano herself. While Nora seems to enjoy the attention that her rare gift brings, she is equally happy playing alone. Typical cat!

Have any other cats taken up unique hobbies?
Gus the Tonkinese cat fits the bill. This fearless feline entered the
Scotland Island Dog Swimming Race, which takes place in Australia every
Christmas Eve. Luckily, while most cats hate the water, some adore it,
and Gus just happened to be one of those rare kitties. As the only
kitty to enter, Gus won gold in the feline cat-egory!

That's cute, but not too helpful! Have cats been trained in any practical ways?
Let's head back over 150 years to the city of Liège in Belgium. Thirty-seven
meowing mail carriers were hired to deliver mail, with letters placed in waterproof
bags around their necks.

THE PURR-FECT PETS

Let's claw our way back to the very beginning and find out when cats became our furry friends!

Where did cats come from?

We all know that living things change over time. It's called evolution. All domestic cats have evolved from one animal ancestor: the North African/ Southwest Asian wildcat.

When did solitary wildcats begin to adapt and live alongside humans?
One line of cats began to interact with ancient farming communities in the Fertile Crescent around 8,000 years ago. Humans tolerated the wildcats, as they patrolled the farmers' crops and kept the rodent population down.

Did these ancient farmers need to convince cats to stay afterward?
Nope! On the whole, cats domesticated themselves. After all, trading in life on the wild side for a handy source of food and shelter seemed like a good idea at the time for these ancient kitties.

Are these the only cats that our kitties today are descended from?
No! A second line of wildcats spread from Egypt to the rest of Africa, Asia, and the Mediterranean. It is thought that this Egyptian cat was friendly and tame, making it an ideal companion!

How did the cat population spread around the world?
Cats were taken aboard ships because they could protect food supplies by taking out rats and mice. Once they reached a foreign port, they'd leap ashore and start a new cat colony.

Were ancient cats just seen as humble mouse-catchers?

No! The ancient Egyptians idolized cats. They were in awe of the cats' ability to protect them from snakes and scorpions, and to keep the grain stores safe from vermin. Over 4,000 years ago, the Egyptians worshipped the cat-headed goddess Mafdet, who was seen as the protector of the pharaoh's, or Egyptian king's, palace. Later, they also worshipped Bastet, who was the feline protector of the home (and an important goddess of Memphis, the ancient Egyptian capital).

How did the ancient Egyptians demonstrate their affection for their feline favorites?

Cats were painted on tomb walls, depicted in bronze statues, and featured on charms, gold rings, and bracelets. When cats died, they were mummified, and their owners shaved off their eyebrows as a sign of mourning. If anyone killed a cat, even if it was accidental, the punishment was death.

Did this passion for cats ever backfire?

At the Battle of Pelusium in 525 BC, the Persian soldiers painted their shields with the image of Bastet and herded cats in front of them, knowing that the Egyptian archers would refuse to shoot their arrows in case they harmed the precious kitties! The plan worked. Around 50,000 Egyptians lost their lives, compared to 7,000 from the Persian army.

Have cats always enjoyed celebrity status throughout history?

No! A moment of silence for the felines of Ypres in Belgium. In the Middle Ages (roughly from the 5th to the 14th or 15th centuries) cats were used to chase away the rodents who nibbled their way through cloth and wool. Soon it was the cat population that was getting out of hand. The Belgians created **Cat Wednesdays**, when frightened felines would be hurled from a church tower. This ruthless tradition continues to this day, but the townsfolk have replaced real cats with stuffed toys!

MEOWS, MYTHS, AND MYSTERIES

Time to take a trip around the world and discover the stories and sagas featuring our feline friends.

Let's start in Europe. Are there any ancient tales to tell?
In Norse mythology, cats were the favorite animal of Freyja, the goddess of luck, love, and fertility. Norwegian Forest cats pulled her chariot and, despite their role as her favorite animal, also gave up their fur to line her gloves!

Do any other places in Europe have feline fables of their own?
The Celts in Scotland used to believe in the Cat Sìth, which means fairy cat. This kitty was a nearly all-black cat (save for a white spot on its chest) the size of a dog, and it featured in many legendary tales. Here's one of them:

One day a farmer was heading home when he stumbled across a procession of cats carrying a coffin and chanting that the King of the Cats was dead. He ran home to tell his wife what he had seen. Upon hearing this story, their own cat sat up and said, "Old Tom is dead? Then I must be king!" The cat walked out of the house, and his owners never saw him again!

Why are cats often connected with witches?

Let's head to Rome in 1233 and have an especially harsh word with Pope Gregory IX. He feared witchcraft and non-Christian activities, so the pope asked an interrogator to hunt down witches' covens. This torturous fellow got confessions from suspected witches, who revealed that new members of the covens were expected to kiss a toad, and a black cat too. The furious pope made an announcement that all cats (especially black ones) were evil. That's one of the reasons why black cats are seen as unlucky to this day!

So black cats aren't unlucky?

Not to humans. Sadly, black cats have to deal with that bad reputation, after all. For centuries afterward, they were seen as witchy . . . at least, in some parts of the world. Over in certain areas of Great Britain and Japan, they're actually considered to be lucky.

Time to take a trip to the ancient Americas.
Did they love cats, or loathe them?

The jaguar was worshipped throughout Mesoamerica (Mexico and Central America) as a divine being. The Mayan civilization believed that the jaguar's night vision allowed the creature to move between worlds. The Mexica (or Aztecs) believed that when the gods created the sun and moon, the jaguar was thrown onto the sacred fire, then came back to life with its fur singed and spotted.

Let's head to Asia! Where would we see cats depicted in Asian cultures? In India, Shashthi, the Hindu goddess of children, is often pictured carrying babies and riding a cat. The famous Puss in Boots also had an Indian twin in a 5th-century folktale.

In ancient China, farmers would make sacrifices to Li Chou, a feline fertility goddess. They believed she protected the crops from troublesome rats and mice. Cats were also important to the beginning of time. According to one story, the gods originally put cats in charge of the world, but because they were more interested in lying around than running things, they nominated people instead!

Why do some Chinese and Japanese stores have statues of cats with their paws raised?

This Maneki-neko figurine first appeared in 17th-century Japan. It's a lucky charm meant to help with money matters. If the left paw is raised, it is supposed to attract customers. If the right paw is waving, then the cat is inviting good fortune and money. You can sometimes spot them with both paws in the air!

How did the Maneki-neko legend begin?

The story goes that a Japanese lord saw a cat waving a paw at him. He was fascinated, so he moved closer to the beckoning cat. At that moment, a lightning bolt hit the place where the lord had previously been standing. The cat's actions had saved the man's life!

So are cats considered lucky in Japan?

I'll say! They even have their own island. Cats were brought to the island Tashirojima nearly 300 hundred years ago to chase the mice away from the islanders' precious silkworms. Over time, Tashirojima's fishing folk came to regard them as good luck, and even built a shrine in their honor. It's now known as Cat Island!

WORLDWIDE WHISKERS

There are over 40 breeds of cat in the world. Pet cats are divided into shorthair and longhair breeds. Let's explore the shorthaired specimens first.

What does the Sphinx cat look like?
It's a medium to large, muscular cat with big, bat-like ears. It looks hairless, although its body is covered in fine fur which feels like suede.

How does this breed behave?
The Sphinx is a real show-off! It will balance, climb, and play tricks for human attention.

ALSO FROM HERE
BOMBAY

What does an Abyssinian look like?
This breed has a strong, agile body, with long, slender legs and large, almond-shaped eyes.

What environment does it enjoy?
It likes space and enjoys climbing, so if you have a home with a lot of cat trees, it'll be in kitty heaven!

What is the Bengal cat's most distinguishing feature?
It's sometimes called a "miniature leopard" because of its super-cool spotted coat. This breed is the result of a cross between a wild Asian leopard cat and a domestic kitty.

What sets this breed apart from other kitties?
Unlike most other cats, the highly curious Bengal loves water! Don't be surprised if it follows you to the bathtub or shower.

What does a Siamese cat look like?

This breed has unique features, including a long, triangular face; bright blue, almond-shaped eyes; a long tapering tail; and a distinctive, dark "mask" on its face.

Why is this cat called "Siamese"?

Legend has it that this breed was used to guard the king of Siam (which is now Thailand). They perched on tall pillars around their owner's throne, then would leap down with their claws at the ready if they felt the king was in danger!

What is unusual about this breed?

Most Manx cats are tail-less! They originally came from the Isle of Man, where their nickname is "stubbin."

What is its personality like?

This gentle and playful cat can be a little dog-like in its behavior! It loves to play fetch and will carry its toys around in its mouth!

MANX

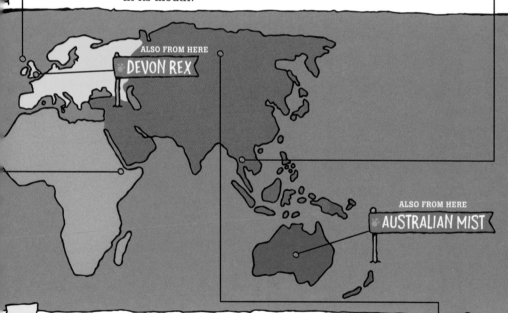

ALSO FROM HERE
DEVON REX

ALSO FROM HERE
AUSTRALIAN MIST

What does this breed look like?

This elegant cat has a silky silver double coat, with dramatic, bright green eyes and an upturned smiley mouth.

What makes the Russian blue special?

Because of its luxurious appearance, this breed has become known as the cat of royalty. Supposedly, these kitties descended from cats kept by the tsars (or kings) of Russia. Queen Victoria of England also kept one after she first met this fabulous furball at an exhibition of cats in 1875.

RUSSIAN BLUE

What do they look like?
These super-soft fluff balls have striking blue eyes and can weigh up to 20 pounds (9 kg).

What is their temper like?
These cats are laid back, friendly, and very tolerant of people!

What is special about this breed?
Maine Coons are known as "gentle giants" and have a heavy coat of long hair to help them endure the freezing winter weather in Maine.

How big can these gentle giants get?
One famous Maine Coon once hit the record books as the world's longest cat. Can you guess how long it was? Turn the page to find the answer!

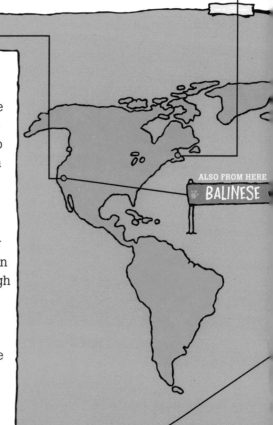

ALSO FROM HERE
BALINESE

What kind of home life does this breed prefer?
Persians are quiet, peaceful cats who like a regular routine. These regal kitties are highly unlikely to scratch the couch, leap onto the kitchen counters, or meow from the top of the refrigerator!

How did the Persian cat make its way out of Iran?
In the 17th century, the Italian composer and world explorer Pietro della Valle fell in love with this breed during his travels through Asia. He first imported these longhaired kitties into Italy in 1626. After cat breeding became popular two centuries later, Persians were finally brought to the United States in the late 19th century.

"Norwegian forest cat" sounds wild! Does their name match their appearance?
This breed has an untamed look, with a dense, waterproof coat; a muscular body; a furry collar ruff; and a fuzzy, swishing tail.

How does this breed behave?
This cat is sweet and affectionate, but is still a hunter at heart. It loves to chase toys and will regularly patrol the house and garden throughout the day.

Why are these cats so special?
White Turkish Angora cats are considered Turkey's national treasure. To preserve this precious kitty, a special breeding program has been set up at the Turkish Ankara Zoo.

How did this breed make it all the way to the U.S.?
In the 1950s, American military personnel stationed in Turkey fell in love with the cats and described them to the folks back home. After much negotiation, the zoo gave a male and female Turkish Angora to Colonel and Mrs. Grant of the U.S. Army in 1962. These cats became the foundations of the breed in the USA.

TURKISH ANGORA

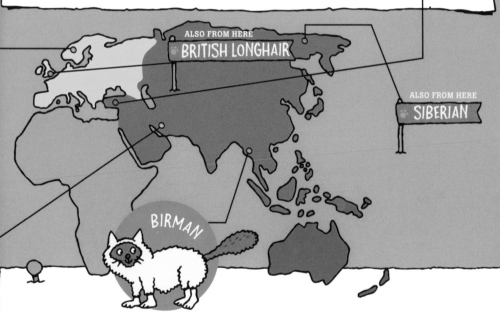

ALSO FROM HERE
BRITISH LONGHAIR

ALSO FROM HERE
SIBERIAN

BIRMAN

What's the low-down on this distinguished kitty?
The Birman is known as the "sacred cat of Burma." It is thought that this breed originally served as companions to the temple priests on the Mount of Lugh.

What is this breed like?
True to their serene origins, these kitties are peaceful and affectionate, but they're also quiet cats that prefer lying about the house.

LITTLE AND LARGE

Cats come in all shapes and sizes. Find your scales, grab a ruler, and check out these fur-midable felines!

How long was the longest cat ever?
A Maine Coon called Stewie measured an incredible four feet (123 cm) from nose to tail. That's about as long as some of you are tall!

Now for the Tallest Cat Contest. Who's purr-fect for this prize?
Let's meet Arcturus Aldebaran Powers. This statuesque Savannah cat reached a height of over 19 inches (48.4 cm).

Which pint-sized pussycat is the smallest cat on record?
Let's hear it for Tinker Toy, a pocket-sized Himalayan-Persian cat.
This small-scale specimen measured just 2.75 inches
(7 cm) tall and 7.5 inches (19 cm) long
when fully grown.

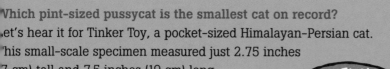
TINKER'S ACTUAL HEIGHT

Which heavyweight kitty cat tops the scales?
We need to head to Australia, which was the home of Himmy,
a 46.8 lb (21.3 kg) tabby cat. That's roughly the same weight as
3 bowling balls! (Entries are now closed in this category. It's not a good
idea to overfeed pets as that makes them extremely unhealthy.)

Now for the Longest Tail Trophy. Who swished by and collected that award? Do you remember Arcturus, the world's tallest cat? Well, his brother, Cygnus, was a record-breaker in his own right. His tail measured a terrific 17.58 inches (44.66 cm), which is about the same as 3 smartphones placed end to end!

Which fuzzy feline wins the Longest Fur Award?
Sophie Smith is the coziest cat ever, with fur measuring
an incredible 10.11 inches (25.68 cm)
at the longest point.

Which curious cat has the Longest Tongue Challenge licked? Well, cats aren't that enthusiastic when it comes to having their tongues measured! But check out Thorin the fluffy ragdoll, who's become an internet sensation with his ridiculously long tongue. It's about the same length as his head!

5 TOES

7 TOES

What are some other unusual records broken by our feline friends?

You usually have five fingers and toes on each hand and foot, right? Well, that's not the case with cats! Kitties usually have five toes on their front paws and four on their back, but some are born with more than that. This condition is called **polydactylism** (*PAH-lee-DACK-till-ism*). Jake, a ginger tabby, took this to an even more claw-some extreme with his 28 toes in total— seven on each paw. Incredible!

FIRST-PRIZE FELINES

Despite the fact that cats sleep up to 15 hours a day, they're incredible athletes. However, there are a few exceptional overachievers! Take a look!

Which cats are the fastest?

With its powerful back legs, the **Egyptian Mau** breed can run as fast as 30 mph (48 km/h). It's got a lot of training to do to catch up with its relative the **cheetah**, who can sprint along at a speedy 60 mph (96 km/h).

FASTEST

What do you call a cat that loves to bowl?

LONGEST JUMP

An alley cat!

Cats are well-known for their leaping skills.
Which daredevil cat has recorded the longest jump?
Let's hear it for Waffle the Warrior Cat who leapt an extraordinary
7 ft (2.13 m). That's longer than your bed!

MOST TRICKS

Independent-minded felines always seem reluctant to perform tricks.
Are there any cats that disprove this belief?
Didga, the skateboarding cat, has hit the headlines by executing a record-breaking
20 tricks in just a minute. The routine includes high fives, rolling over, spinning,
and performing a "hippie jump" on her board.

FELINE
HALL OF
FAME

Who's in the running for a mouse-catching medal?

Towser would certainly make it onto the podium. She lived for 24 years in a Scottish whiskey factory, and over that time she caught an estimated 28,899 mice! A bronze statue was built in her memory, and Towser's paw print was stamped on the label of a special whiskey bottled in her honor!

TOWSER

BEST MOUSE-CATCHER

Which cats wins the Mom of the Year award?

It's a tie! A Burmese/Siamese cat from Oxfordshire, U.K., gave birth to a litter of 19 kittens in 1970. (Most mama cats have between 4 and 6 kittens at a time.) Meanwhile, a Texan tabby called Dusty produced a grand total of 420 kittens in her lifetime.

BUSIEST MOM

Who was the world's oldest cat?

Most cats only live to be about 15 years old (though it really depends on the breed). However, Creme Puff is the oldest cat ever recorded, having lived from August 3, 1967, to August 6, 2005. Can you work out how long that is? Over 38 years!

OLDEST KITTY

Which kitties have survived some extreme circumstances?

Introducing Andy, owned by U.S. Senator Ken Myer, who fell 200 feet (61 m) from a 16th-floor apartment . . . and survived! Honorable mention goes to a fellow feline survivor who was rescued from the rubble of a collapsed building 80 days after an earthquake struck Taiwan. Happily, the lucky cat made a full recovery, but might've lost one of its nine lives!

EXIT

CATS ON THE GO

Not all felines stay at home and slumber. Some cats step up to the plate and go out to work. Let's find out about these productive pussycats!

We know that cats are experienced mouse-catchers. Did they turn this talent into an actual job?

In the U.K., cats were employed at post offices to get rid of mail-nibbling mice. The original three cats to fill this duty were rewarded with only 1 shilling (almost $2) per week, which was used to buy food for them. That's only $2 for all three cats! In the U.S., postal clerk George W. Cook, who took care of New York's army of mouser postal cats, celebrated his 54th work anniversary in 1904 by throwing a banquet in honor of his feline coworkers, funded by the government. The guest list included two sergeant cats called Bill and Richard, as well as 57 patrol cats.

Have cats been used in any dangerous missions?
Félicette, a French feline, had a job that was literally "out of this world"!
After months of training, she became the first cat launched into space in 1963.
Her brain activity, heart rate, and breathing were monitored throughout the
13-minute flight, which provided invaluable data for the space scientists.

Let's get back to Earth! What other valuable jobs have cats done?

One saved a railway line! In 2007, a nine-mile (14.5 km) rural railway line in Japan faced closure because of low profits and passenger numbers. The rail company made a stray cat called Tama honorary stationmaster for one of its stations, and visitors flocked to see her. The local governor described her as a "superstar of tourism," and Tama was promoted to vice-president of the rail firm and given the title of "honorable eternal stationmaster"!

That sounds like important work! Which cat enjoyed more trivial tasks?

In the 1930s, British writer Elinor Glyn was famous for dining out with her cat Candide draped around her shoulders as a fashion accessory!

Let's fast-forward to today! Do cats have any useful assignments?
If you paid a visit to the Royal London Hospital, you might bump into Mr. London Meow. He's a therapy cat who comforts patients by letting them pet him. Over at UC San Francisco's medical center in California, rescue kitty Duke Ellington Morris brightens up an intensive care unit in his role as a cat therapist.

We have sniffer dogs at airports and in police departments.
Have cats ever been used in this way?
Recent research has found that a cat's sense of smell could be four times sharper than a dog's. With proper coaching, cats could be used to find missing people, sniff out bombs, and even detect medical issues. A cat could be an expert in this field with its climbing and balancing skills, ability to squeeze into small spaces, and that sharp feline nose.

Which heroic cats should win bravery awards?

There are many tales of fearless felines. Take a look!

TARA

This courageous cat was put to the test when a dog suddenly attacked her four-year-old owner. With lightning-fast cat reflexes, Tara fought the dog off and saved her human's life!

BABY

This timid tabby saved its family's life when it woke its owner by jumping up and down in his lap. A fire had started in an upstairs bedroom, but due to Baby's actions, everyone in the house survived.

PUDDING

This quick-witted cat pulled his owner out of a diabetic coma by leaping up onto her chest, biting her nose, and patting her face. What makes this story even more impressive is that it had only been a few hours since Pudding's owner had adopted him from an animal shelter.

Where could I go to see cats at work?

Do you like coffee? How about a slice of cake, or a cookie? Let's take a trip to a cat café. The Austrians claim to have opened the first one in 1912, and now there are over 150 in Japan alone! Cat cafés are especially popular in areas where apartments ban pet ownership, so city dwellers can come and relax, play with the kitties, and forget about the stress of urban life!

PAMPERED PUSSYCATS AND FAMOUS FELINES

It's time to take a look at some of the planet's most well-known and well-loved cats! How many have you heard of?

Cats have clawed their way into most sections of our society. Have there ever been politically inclined felines?

The 16th President of the United States, Abraham Lincoln, was passionate about his two cats, called Tabby and Dixie. He once fed Tabby at the table during a White House banquet, much to the embarrassment of the First Lady. Lincoln was unrepentant. "If the gold fork was good enough for former President James Buchanan," he said, "I think it is good enough for Tabby."

Have any other political leaders enjoyed the company of cats?
In the U.K., Larry the cat is the Chief Mouser at 10 Downing Street, the Prime Minister's official residence. This rescue stray cat soon earned the nickname "Lazy Larry," as he preferred napping to hunting, so it was left to government ministers to chase away any mice!

Which stylish kitty is queen of the catwalk?
That title belongs to Choupette, the cat owned by the famous fashion designer
Karl Lagerfeld. This pampered pussycat has its own Instagram account, regularly
features in glossy magazines, and has inspired makeup lines and handbags.
To help her deal with this exhausting lifestyle, Choupette is cared for by two
minders, a bodyguard, a doctor, and a personal chef!

That's one spoiled kitty cat! Does she top the rich list?
Choupette's financial dealings are a closely guarded secret.
But we do know of a feline called Blackie who inherited an eye-popping
$12.5 million (£7 million) from his multi-millionaire owner, Ben Rea.
In his will Mr. Rea ignored his family and split his wealth between
his pet, cat charities, his gardener, his mechanic, and his plumber!

That's one lucky cat! Would you say it's the luckiest?

That honor goes to Oscar, also known as "Unsinkable Sam," who survived not one, not two, but three shipwrecks in World War II! After the German Bismarck sank in 1941, its ship cat Oscar was rescued by the British crew of *HMS Cossack*. After a few months of serving the *HMS Cossack*, Oscar (recently renamed Sam) survived the torpedoing and sinking of his new home and wound up on the aircraft carrier *HMS Ark Royal*. Less than a month later, the *Ark Royal* was torpedoed by another German U-boat. After surviving even this, Oscar/Sam left his fantastic naval career for safety in a retirement home for sailors in Northern Ireland.

Talking of Oscars, which film star felines have made it big in the movies?

Mrs. Norris, the cat character in the Harry Potter films, was played by not one, but at least four Maine coon actor cats. The four main cats were cast for their different skill sets: Alanis was an expert at keeping still, Pebbles could walk then stop on a certain spot, Maximus was trained to jump onto a fellow actor's shoulders, and Cornilus could sit and stare on command.

ALANIS PEBBLES MAXIMUS CORNILUS

How have cats achieved fame in the scientific community?

Let me introduce you to Little Nicky. He's the first cloned-to-order pet cat. Nicky's owner paid a Californian cloning laboratory for a kitty that was the exact duplicate of her previous pet. However, scientists and animal rights advocates frowned on this, as the cloning process is still experimental and risky, and whether it's right to clone animals is still a hot topic for debate.

Which cats have become internet sensations?

The first cat video on YouTube, a thirty-second clip of a cat named Pajamas, was posted in 2005. Since then the world has been fanatical for feline footage. The original video of the Keyboard Cat, an early internet feline celebrity, was posted two years later and quickly gained millions of views. Cat memes, like Grumpy Cat, took the internet by storm in the 2010s, and cats like Nala, a kitty with her own Instagram, can easily amass millions of followers today.

HAPPY CATS!

Want a feline friend? Check out these tips first!

How much care do these independent critters need?

Any pet needs daily attention, and some feline breeds get very anxious if they are left alone all day. Don't forget that a cat can live for at least 15 years, so adopting a kitten is a long-term commitment.

What do I need to consider before choosing a cat?

1. Is the cat suitable for the whole family? It may be nervous around noisy kids, or a family member may suffer from allergies.

2. Do you want a kitten or a cat? A kitten will need extra supervision as it masters litter box training, and it requires four small meals each day.

3. Cats are natural hunters, so you need to be ready for the odd mouse dropped onto your doormat, scratched furniture, and cat hair!

4. Although home-loving cats are happy to stay safe inside, free-roaming felines that have gotten used to roaming around a garden may find it hard to adjust to an indoor lifestyle. You may wish to provide it with an enclosed outdoor "cat patio," or give it a brightly colored collar with a bell.

What equipment will I need?
Here's a cat-care kit list!

CAT TOYS

FEEDING BOWLS

Wide, shallow feeding and water bowls so your cats' whiskers won't hit the sides.

CAT BED

A bed. Remember, cats sleep for up to 16 hours a day!

COLLAR

CAT LITTER

A reflective collar, so that drivers can spot your cat at night if your cat likes roaming the wild outdoors.

A litter box, litter, and a pooper-scooper, so your cat can do its business and so you can clean up after it. Ideally, this should be placed away from your cats' eating and sleeping areas.

OPER OOPER

LITTER BOX

All cats shed hairs, so a brush will be needed for a weekly grooming session.

CAT BRUSH

Cats like to keep their claws in tip-top shape, so a scratching post would be useful (and might save your furniture!).

CAT CARRIER

A safe and secure cat carrier to bring your cat home, and for making trips to the vet for your cat's vaccinations, health checks, and possibly a microchip (which is a permanent form of ID, in case your pet ever gets lost).

SCRATCHING POST

Some toys!

How should I cater for a cat? What do they like to eat?
Cats are obligate carnivores. That means they need to eat meat and can't survive on a vegetarian diet. Shop for a small selection of food to see what your cat prefers, and make sure there is fresh water handy at all times.

What is the best way to find the right cat?
You could start with cat shelters and rescue centers. The staff at these facilities will work hard to make sure that you find the right cat for your lifestyle and environment. They might visit your home, and will share knowledge about your cat and give pet-care advice and support.

What if I want a cat that's purely a specific breed?
Well, some rescue centers house purebred cats (a cat of one specific breed, or a pedigreed cat) too. You can also make an appointment with a registered breeder to arrange a visit to see a litter. The breeder should keep their cats in a clean and spacious environment, and when you visit, pay close attention to the behavior of the mother and kittens to make sure they're comfortable and well taken care of.

It sounds impossible to choose one kitten from a litter!
What should I check for?

- Is the kitten lively and active?

- Has it got a healthy coat, bright eyes, and clean ears?

- Will the breeder or shelter check the kitten for any disorders that other cats of the same breed often suffer from, and ensure that your soon-to-be pet is vaccinated and wormed (given shots and medicine to keep it from getting sick)?

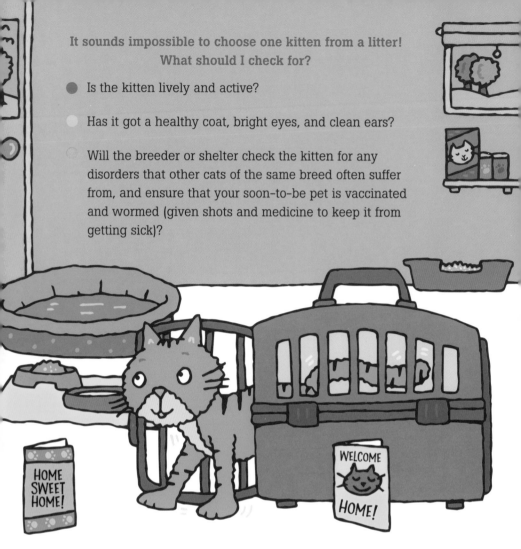

HOME SWEET HOME!

WELCOME HOME!

So, I've chosen my purr-fect pet, and we're heading home!
How should I settle my cat in?

1 Prepare one quiet room with food, water, a litter box, and somewhere warm to sleep. Your cat will feel safe in here while it gets used to its new home.

2 Put the cat carrier down, open it, then leave your new pet to explore. Cats often like to hide when they arrive somewhere new, so an empty cardboard box might be a thoughtful addition to this room.

3 As your cat starts to explore, make sure all doors leading to the great outdoors and windows are shut. If you want your cat to be an outdoor cat, keep it indoors for at least two weeks, then let it out just before a meal. If your cat is hungry, some food will coax it back inside!

WELCOME HOME, KITTY!

Your cat is happy, settled, and part of the family. Here are some questions that might pop up as you observe your new fluffy friend!

Why does my cat twitch in its sleep?
It's nothing to worry about—your cat is just dreaming!

Why does my cat sit on newspaper?
Simple! It's soft, it's warm, and if you're reading it, they get plenty of attention!

My cat chatters its teeth when it sees a bird. Why does it do this?
There are several theories:

- A cat's instinct is to rapidly vibrate its jaw, because it wants to catch the bird and dispatch it quickly.

- The cat is frustrated, as it can't get to the bird.

- The cat is trying to copy a bird's chirps, so that the bird relaxes and the cat can pounce!

- It's excited!

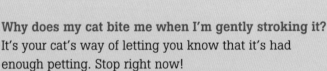

Why does my cat bite me when I'm gently stroking it?
It's your cat's way of letting you know that it's had enough petting. Stop right now!

Why does my cat pounce on my ankles?
Your ankles are a moving target at exactly the right height for a playful kitty cat! Remember, your cat is a mighty hunter, so pouncing is a form of play that fits its nature as a predator. The best way to tame this mighty beast is to buy new toys to occupy your fun-loving fluffball.

Hope you're full of feline facts and tabby-cat tips!
You're paw-some!

CHECK OUT ALL OF THE FANTASTIC FACTS IN THIS SENSATIONAL SERIES!